DATE DUE			

A New True Book

CANYONLANDS

NATIONAL PARK

By David Petersen

CHILDRENS PRESS ®

CHICAGO

Canyonlands National Park
is in southeastern Utah.

Library of Congress Cataloging-in-Publication Data

Petersen, David.
   Canyonlands / by David Petersen.
     p.   cm. — (A New true book)
   Includes index.
   Summary: Describes the formation and features of
the canyons created by the force of the Colorado and
Green Rivers in Utah.
   ISBN 0-516-01132-4
   1. Canyonlands National Park (Utah)—Juvenile
literature. [1. Canyonlands National Park (Utah).
2. National parks and reserves.] I. Title.
II. Title: Canyonlands.
F832.C37P38 1992
979.2'59—dc20   91-35274
                             CIP
                             AC

PHOTO CREDITS

© Reinhard Brucker—6 (left and right), 16, 20 (bottom right), 38 (bottom right), 39 (right), 44 (center and right)

© John Elk III—39 (left)

© Virginia R. Grimes—19, 20 (bottom left), 25

© National Park Service—40 (right)

© Jerry Hennen—26 (left), 29, 38 (bottom left), 43 (top left)

Historical Pictures Service—41 (right)

Journalism Services—© Dave Brown, Cover, 6 (center), 8, 11, 12, 31, 34

© Kirkendall/Spring—2, 43 (bottom right), 45

© Dan Peha—35 (2 photos), 37, 38 (top)

© Chip and Rosa Maria de la Cueva Peterson—7 (left), 30, 44 (left)

© Branson Reynolds—24, 27 (bottom right), 41 (left)

Root Resources—© Stephen Trimble, 13; © George Doerner, 20 (top left and right)

Tom Stack & Associates—© Manfred Gottschalk, 7 (right), 33; © Stewart M. Green, 22; © Wendy Shattil/Bob Rozinski, 27 (top left); © Don and Esther Phillips, 27 (top right); © Robert Winslow, 40 (left)

SuperStock International, Inc.—© Sal Maimone, 18

TSW-CLICK/Chicago—© Tom Till, 4; © Willard Clay, 26 (right)

Valan—© Prof. R.C. Simpson, 27 (bottom left); © John Cancalosi, 43 (bottom left); © B. Templeman, 43 (top right)

Map—15

Cover—"The Maze," a twisting complex of canyons carved from multicolored layers of sandstone, is located in a remote area of Canyonlands National Park.

Project Editor: Fran Dyra
Design: Margrit Fiddle

TABLE OF CONTENTS

STRANGE ROCK FORMATIONS

Canyonlands National Park, in Utah, is like no other national park in America. At Canyonlands, there are no lodges or motels, no showers, no coin laundries. There are no restaurants and no souvenir shops.

All Canyonlands has is 527 square miles (1,365 square kilometers) of almost bottomless canyons, and lots of huge, strange-looking rocks.

The Doll House, Turks Head, and Candlestick Tower (left to right).
Wind-blown sand helped to carve Canyonlands' rock formations.

Many of the rock formations at Canyonlands are named for things they look like:

The Doll House   Lizard Rock
Bagpipe Butte   Candlestick Tower
Cathedral Point   Turks Head
Chimney Rock   Peekaboo Spring
                     Paul Bunyans Potty

Let's explore this wilderness of rock.

STORIES WRITTEN IN STONE

It helps to think of Canyonlands as a giant layer cake cut into three big pieces. The tool nature has used to cut the cake is running water—the Colorado and Green rivers.

The Colorado River (left) and Green River flow through deep, rocky canyons as they pass through Canyonlands.

The different colored bands on the canyon walls were formed by separate layers of sand laid down at different times.

The cliff walls of the river canyons are the cut edges that divide the cake into three pieces. In these exposed edges, you can see the separate layers of the giant stone cake.

8

These layers tell the history of Canyonlands.

Canyonlands didn't become a national park until 1964. But its story began millions of years ago.

Way back then, Canyonlands did not look like it does now. It had no deep canyons, no steep cliffs, no big rocks that looked like lizards or bagpipes. Back then, Canyonlands was the flat bottom of a shallow sea.

When this ancient sea dried up, only a layer of sand was left to show where the water had been.

Later, another sea came, flooding the same area again. It too dried up, leaving a second layer of sand covering the first.

This flooding and drying happened many times. And each time, a new layer of sand was deposited. Some of these sand layers were white or buff. Others were red, orange, or pink. This gave the layers colored stripes.

Very slowly, under their own weight, the billions of sand grains became fused together. The result is *sandstone*.

Some rock formations have layers made of different kinds of rock. This tower is made of sandstone and limestone, a rock made from millions of tiny animal shells.

Eroded sandstone rock formations

Compared to other kinds of rock, sandstone is soft. Because of its softness, it is easily *eroded*. Erosion is a natural force that shapes the surface of the earth. Two important tools of erosion are water and wind.

As water from rain and melting snow puddles flows over sandstone, it dissolves the natural cement binding the sand grains together. In this way, tons of sand is loosened and swept away into the powerful waters of the Colorado and Green rivers

The Green River (left) empties into the Colorado River (right) in Canyonlands.

each year. This suspended sand is what makes the rivers run red.

The fast-moving, sand-filled rivers are like liquid sandpaper. As water rushes along, the suspended sand grinds away at the river channels. This grinding causes even more sand grains to be loosened. More sandstone is thus eroded. And the river canyons are slowly carved deeper and wider.

This is how, over a *very*

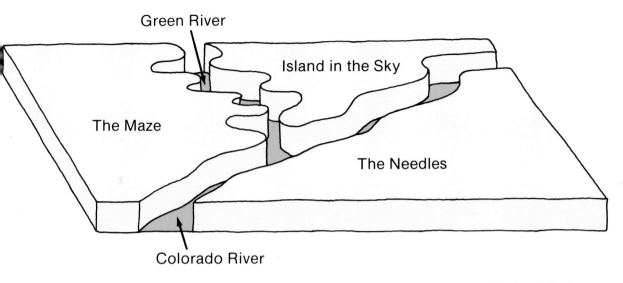

Green River

Island in the Sky

The Maze

The Needles

Colorado River

A map of Canyonlands National Park

long time, the Colorado
and Green rivers have cut
the deep canyons that
divide the Canyonlands
into three big pieces.

In addition to the two
big rivers and their
canyons, other streams

have left hundreds of smaller canyons crisscrossing all through Canyonlands. When two canyons are cut close together, a wall of sandstone is left standing between them. There are

This part of Island in the Sky is called Monument Basin.

many such walls at Canyonlands. Some of the walls are very thin and jagged on top. They look a little like fish fins. No wonder they're called *fins*.

But water is not the only tool of erosion. Wind also works to erode sandstone.

When the wind blows, it picks up loose, dry sand grains and hurls them against the canyon walls and fins. The blowing sand eats away at

everything in its path. In
this way, wind has helped
to smooth, round, and
shape the rock formations
of Canyonlands.

In some places, water
and the other forces of
erosion have "drilled" large

holes completely through
sandstone walls and fins.
The spans of rock across
the tops of these big
holes are called *arches*.

The arches at Canyonlands
are named for the things

Mesa Arch looks like a giant bridge.

Some Canyonlands arches (clockwise from top left): Angel, Wedding Ring, Washer Woman, Wooden Shoe. Can you see these things in the arches?

they look like:

Angel	Wooden Shoe
Castle	Fortress
Wedding Ring	Horsehoof
Washer Woman	Caterpillar

You need a good imagination to see some of these things in the arches. But a few, like Wooden Shoe Arch, look *exactly* like their names.

The three districts of Canyonlands are also named for their natural features. Their names are The Needles, Island in the Sky, and The Maze. Let's explore all three, one at a time.

The Needles are tall sandstone columns formed by erosion.

THE NEEDLES

The Needles District covers the southeastern third of Canyonlands. It is separated from the other two districts by the canyon of the Colorado River.

The "needles" for which this place is named are tall, thin columns of orange-and-white sandstone.

Near the center of The Needles is a campground called Devil's Kitchen. In

Banded rock formations in Devil's Kitchen

spite of its spooky name, Devil's Kitchen is a very pretty place.

To see the best views in The Needles, you have to put on your walking shoes. There are many trails.

Some are steep and long. Others are easy and short. One interesting trail leads to a place called Pothole Point. The hike to Pothole Point and back is just over 1 mile (1.6 kilometers). You walk over smooth sandstone, called *slickrock*.

Water running off slickrock after a rainstorm

Some water-filled potholes are almost perfectly round.
Others are irregular in shape.

Over the ages, water
has eroded shallow "dishes"
into the surface of the
slickrock. These depressions
are called *potholes*.

Rain and melting snow
fill the potholes with water.
Most pothole pools are
small and shallow. Others
are very large.

Mule deer, lizards, foxes, and cactus wrens
(clockwise from top left) are some of
the animals that live in Canyonlands.

Because Canyonlands is
desert country, pothole water
is very important to wildlife.
Birds, deer, lizards, foxes,
and other wild creatures
visit the potholes to drink.

ISLAND IN THE SKY

The northeastern third of Canyonlands is called Island in the Sky. It is a *mesa*, or high, flat area. It rises more than 2,000 feet (600 meters) above the Colorado River. Its sides are steep cliffs.

You don't have to do a lot of walking to enjoy the best views at Island in the Sky. A paved road winds throughout the mesa. The road leads to many scenic overlooks.

About 1,200 feet (370 meters) below the Island, a broad, flat sandstone bench juts out like a giant step. It is called the White Rim. Another 1,000 feet

Views from Island in the Sky reveal many miles of canyons and rock formations.

White Rim and the Colorado River canyons, seen from Green River Overlook

(300 meters) below the White Rim, runs the Colorado River. Such giant scenery makes people feel as tiny as ants.

On a clear day, you can

see *three* mountain ranges from Island in the Sky. To the south are the Abajos. To the southwest rise the Henrys. And nearest, in the east, are the La Sals.

From this point on the White Rim Road, you can see the La Sal Mountains in the distance.

THE MAZE

A maze is a confusing
network of passages. That
is why the most remote
district of Canyonlands has
been named The Maze.
Occupying the western
third of Canyonlands, The
Maze is a jumble of
sandstone canyons
hundreds of feet deep.

The Maze is one of the
wildest, loneliest places in
the world. To explore The
Maze, you must travel by

The Maze as seen from the air

foot, on horseback, or in a
four-wheel-drive vehicle.
The roads are unpaved,
bumpy, and dusty. There
are no gas stations, no
water, no toilets. You must
bring along everything you

33

The canyons of The Maze show the multicolored
sandstone layers of Canyonlands rocks.

might need. And in order
to keep this beautiful
place clean and natural,
you must carry out your
own trash.

Exploring The Maze is
one of the two greatest
adventures in Canyonlands.
The other is river boating.

River boating is
a great way to
see the canyons
of the Green and
Colorado rivers.

THE RIVERS

Looking down from high overlooks in The Maze, The Needles, and Island in the Sky gives you a bird's-eye view of Canyonlands. To get a fish's-eye view, you can float down the Green or Colorado river in a raft or a dory boat.

Safe, guided float trips leave every day from the towns of Moab and Green River, Utah. The Colorado

River boats must plunge through one rapid after another.
There is no turning back!

River is big and has huge,
foaming rapids. Floating
on the river is a very
exciting way to see
Canyonlands!

The Native Americans who lived in Canyonlands long ago stored grain in rock structures, some of which they built in openings high up in the canyon walls.

YOUR TRIP TO CANYONLANDS

The first people to see Canyonlands were the Native Americans. We know they lived there long ago by the things they left behind. They left the ruins of stone cliff houses. They left painted pictures and

Some of the rock pictures and carvings in Canyonlands may be 3,000 years old.

Native American rock art. The colorful pictograph on the left is known as The All-American Man. The pictograph above depicts The Harvest Scene.

carvings on the canyon walls. And they left stone arrow points scattered here and there. All of these help make Canyonlands more interesting.

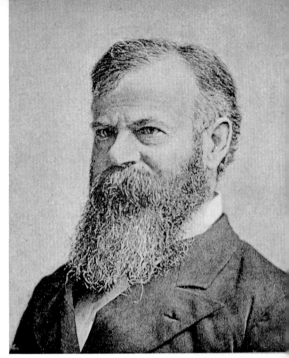

John Wesley Powell explored the canyons of the Green and Colorado rivers in 1869. He described the strange rock formations of Canyonlands.

Next came explorers and trappers. They left nothing behind. But some of them, like John Wesley Powell, described the deep canyons and weird rock formations in their journals.

41

Later came the land surveyors and miners. They took uranium ore and other valuable minerals from the canyons. They left a mess of rusting machinery, scarred earth, and bad roads.

Today, the prehistoric Indians, trappers, and miners are gone. Now, people come to Canyonlands National Park to enjoy the scenery, and to hike, camp, boat, and take pictures.

In summer, temperatures

Visitors explore Canyonlands' rivers by boat.
They hike along the trails to explore historic
ruins (top right), and they camp out in
tents (above). There are many opportunities
for photographers to take spectacular pictures.

down in the canyons are
often above 100° F (38° C).
Winter in Canyonlands
can be cold and windy.
Sometimes it even snows.
The best seasons to

Colorful
flowers bloom
in the rocky
wilderness of
Canyonlands.

visit Canyonlands are spring and fall. But visit whenever you can. Canyonlands National Park is not a place to be missed. It is a western wonderland. It's almost as much fun as going to the moon—and a lot closer.

Druid Arch. Many areas of Canyonlands can be visited only by hikers, since there are few paved roads.

WORDS YOU SHOULD KNOW

ancient (AIN • shent) — very old; from long ago

buff (BUFF) — a dark-yellow color

canyon (CAN • yun) — a long, narrow valley that has high cliffs on each side

channel (CHAN • il) — the bed of a river or a stream

cliff (KLIFF) — a high, steep rock face that goes down sharply with little or no slope

crisscross (KRISS • krawss) — to cross back and forth over

deposit (dih • PAH • zit) — to lay down; to drop

depression (dih • PRESH • un) — a dent; a low place or a hollow

desert (DEH • zert) — a dry area that gets very little rainfall

dissolve (dih • ZAHLV) — to melt in a liquid; to make or become liquid

district (DISS • trikt) — an area; a place with certain boundaries

erosion (ih • ROH • zjun) — the wearing away of the land, caused by the action of wind and water

explore (ex • PLOR) — to travel to new places to find out what is there

formation (for • MAY • shun) — the way a thing is shaped or put together; something that is shaped in a certain way

fused (FYOOZD) — joined together

imagination (ih • maj • ih • NAY • shun) — the ability to picture things in the mind

jagged (JAG • id) — having notches and sharp points, like the teeth of a saw

journal (JER • nil) — a written record of what happens each day

maze (MAYZ) — a confusing network of passages

mesa (MAY • sa) — a high, flat area with steep sides, like a table

rapids (RAP • idz) — stretches of a stream that are shallow and strewn with rocks, so that the water runs fast and rough

ruins (ROO • inz) — the fallen-down or decayed remains of old
   buildings
scenic (SEE • nik) — having interesting or beautiful scenery
souvenir (soo • ven • EER) — something that is kept as a reminder
   of some event
surveyor (ser • VAY • er) — a person who measures the land and
   marks out boundaries
suspended (sus • PEN • did) — held in a liquid, but not dissolved
uranium ore (yoo • RAY • nee • um OR) — a mineral that is found
   in the ground and is used to make fuel for nuclear
   power plants
wonderland (WUN • der • land) — a place that is full of strange and
   beautiful sights

INDEX

About the Author

David Petersen is a writer and teacher. He lives in southwestern Colorado and visits Canyonlands National Park often.